THEN & NOW

PRINCETON

Best wishes,
"Then & Now
and Always,

Richard D. Smith

THEN & NOW

PRINCETON

Richard D. Smith

This book is dedicated to the memory of Gail Stern (1950–2006), former director of the Historical Society of Princeton. She facilitated my previous two books for Arcadia Publishing and championed this one before her passing. She brought me on as guest curator of the exhibition Princeton Recollections, another wonderful experience. She was a cherished friend, collaborator, and encourager to me and to so many others. We remember the "then," Gail. Here's a "now" for you.

Copyright © 2007 by Richard D. Smith
ISBN 978-0-7385-4946-0

Library of Congress control number: 2006932975

Published by Arcadia Publishing
Charleston SC, Chicago IL, Portsmouth NH, San Francisco CA

Printed in the United States of America

For all general information contact Arcadia Publishing at:
Telephone 843-853-2070
Fax 843-853-0044
E-mail sales@arcadiapublishing.com
For customer service and orders:
Toll-Free 1-888-313-2665

Visit us on the Internet at www.arcadiapublishing.com

On the front cover: Shown here is Nassau Street. (Vintage image courtesy of the Historical Society of Princeton; contemporary image courtesy of Richard D. Smith.)

On the back cover: Please see page 41. (Courtesy of the Historical Society of Princeton.)

CONTENTS

ACKNOWLEDGMENTS

Just as no one person builds a town like Princeton, no one person could create a book like this.

My sincere thanks to the Historical Society of Princeton, which has allowed the photographs in its collection to be used for *Princeton*, and to my friends and collaborators there, Eileen Morales (the collection's curator), Jeanette Cafaro, Marcia Lopez, Karin Morse, Barbara Webb, and, of course, the late Gail Stern; Shirley Satterfield; Ric Endersby and the Princeton History Project, whose Princeton Pictorial Archives is now part of the historical society's overall photograph collection; Wanda Gunning and Constance Greiff for sharing their encyclopedic personal knowledge of Princeton history and architecture; Princeton University staff photographer Denise Applewhite for her sage technical advice; Pamala Zill, my efficient and enthusiastic field photography assistant; Joseph W. Felcone for years of encouraging my research into 18th-century Princeton history; Mary Guimond, manager of the Princeton University Department of Ecology and Evolutionary Biology, for use of the department's image scanner; Department of Rare Books and Special Collections, Princeton University Library; my long-suffering Arcadia editor Erin Stone and long-suffering publisher Tiffany Howe for their professionalism, patience and support; my copy editor Heather O'Neal; and for their patience and support, thanks to all my good friends, not the least of whom is my mother, Mae W. Smith.

In addition to the historical society archives and the personal knowledge of Wanda Gunning and Constance Greiff, I found two sources to be especially valuable as basic references: *Princeton Architecture: A Pictorial History of Town and Campus* by Constance M. Greiff, Mary W. Gibbons, and Elizabeth G. C. Menzies published in Princeton by Princeton University Press, 1967, and *The Campus Guide: Princeton University* by Raymond P. Rhinehart published in New York by Princeton Architectural Press, 1999.

All archival images, unless otherwise noted, are from the collection of the Historical Society of Princeton.

INTRODUCTION

Benjamin Franklin is said to have written that New Jersey was a barrel tapped at both ends. Like many of Franklin's observations, this quip was is accurate as it is witty. Located immediately between New York and Philadelphia, New Jersey was oriented toward and used by both of these great American cities.

But it could be just as truly said that New Jersey—and Princeton, one of its most famous towns—were barrels filled at both ends.

The original crown land grants in New Jersey divided the colony not north and south but into eastern and western provinces. Largely because of this, New Jersey was settled from its edges inward.

This was strikingly the case in Princeton, which is situated very nearly in the geographical center of the state. What is the central Princeton borough and the surrounding Princeton township were crossed for centuries by Lenni Lenapes of the Delaware Native American nation traveling between the Raritan River (at modern-day New Brunswick) and the Delaware River (at today's state capital of Trenton). But the first European settlements came in the late 1600s on the outskirts of modern Princeton, along Stony Brook to the west and along the Millstone (near today's neighboring town of Kingston) to the east. Only as the 1700s progressed, did western and eastern expansion meet—and complete—in what is today's Princeton.

The Stony Brook settlers on the west were largely members of the Society of Friends (Quakers). On the east and in neighboring areas came people of English and Dutch descent. The College of New Jersey, founded in 1746 in Elizabeth, came here in 1756 and, of course, eventually became Princeton University. Over the years, virtually every nationality and race has arrived to make a home in Princeton and help the community thrive.

Perhaps because of Princeton's varied but significant role in American histories, social, economic, political, and educational, and because of its picturesque nature, we are fortunate to have a wealth of photographic views of the town from the mid-1800s to the present. To identify an intriguing "then" archival image and to locate and photograph its "now" has been a fascinating and often delightfully surprising process. Princeton is a town that has changed greatly in some ways and scarcely changed in others.

In the first chapter, Princeton is considered as a town that grew up not around a village green, courthouse square, or harbor but along a stagecoach road, the King's Highway, a former Native American trail and today's Routes 27 and 206. The next chapter will reveal that often in Princeton it is not the house but the background that changes. Princeton was founded by religious people and has evolved as a multicultural town, so in the third chapter, a few of its many places of worship are shown. Of course, Princeton is known internationally for the university situated here; its seemingly eternal but actually ever-changing campus is revealed. The final chapter is devoted to the project that most changed the face of Princeton's downtown, Palmer Square.

How has Princeton changed the most? The answer is not the usual replies about "growth" or "loss of old neighborhoods." Princeton has had its share of development and preservation issues during the incredible post–World War II growth of the central New Jersey region, but it has generally handled them well. My answer, after months of crossing streets, traversing the campus, and scrambling up and down hills to take the "now" photographs for *Princeton*, is traffic and trees.

In the 1960s and 1970s, there were appeals for the creation of a beltway around Princeton to funnel the growing traffic on Routes 27 and 206 away from Nassau Street and Princeton's downtown. Opponents of the beltway successfully argued that it would enable development in the surrounding rural countryside. Whatever the case, development came to the region anyway. Nassau Street is now often a bottleneck on the roads between New Brunswick and Trenton. Trying to stand exactly where a century-old photograph was taken without a car fender or truck panel intruding (or without getting hit) has been a challenge.

But the traffic eventually moves on, and the scene opens again. Trees do not move. Contrary to widespread conception, there are today many more trees in New Jersey than in bygone days when much of the land was cleared for farming and for wood needed for fuel as well as building. So, it has been more productive to shoot "now" views during fall and winter when leaves do not utterly mask the view. But sometimes tree growth is very much part of Princeton's "then" and "now" story. There is no denying that the aesthetic planting of trees has made Princeton as lovely and parklike as it is historic.

ALONG THE KING'S HIGHWAY

COMMERCE AND TRANSPORTATION

Even when its main thoroughfare of Nassau Street was dusty or muddy, Princeton prospered during the horse-and-buggy era. Only the American Revolution, the economic panic of 1837, and the Great Depression of 1929 seriously slowed its vitality.

11

The earliest occupation in Princeton, as in much of Colonial America, was farming. This artist's conception shows the fields and orchards of Thomas Clark as they probably appeared just before the morning of January 3, 1777, when the Battle of Princeton was fought here. This historic site was saved from development by concerned citizens and now benefits grateful modern visitors, such as this father and his sons.

An early wooden bridge over the Stony Brook was a casualty of the Battle of Princeton, partially destroyed to slow British reinforcements coming back along the King's Highway. It was replaced in 1792 by the bridge that still carries traffic on what is today Route 206. Worth's Mill stood for many years on the western bank, using the brook's power to turn its wheels, but only one of its walls remains today.

The growing of crops necessitated the building of mills to grind wheat and corn or to press apples into cider. This mill near Kingston was built on the aptly-named Millstone River and along the King's Highway (modern-day Route 27). It is now a private residence (shown in the modern photograph from a reverse angle to the archival image). In the 1960s, a bypass for Route 27 was built above the mill, leaving the original alignment over the 18th-century bridge to end in the building's driveway.

An outdoor market once stood in Nassau Street near the intersection of today's South Tulane Street and adjacent to the site of the famous 18th-century tavern known as Hudibras (which in its last service was called the City Hotel). The archival photograph predates 1871, when the market was torn down.

Nassau Street, the main street of Princeton, was slow to improve after its Colonial stage line days, as shown in this rarely published 19th-century view. It was not completely macadamized until 1896 and not paved in asphalt until 1915.

At least three buildings have stood on Nassau Street at the corner of Witherspoon Street. This store replaced an earlier structure in 1850. It was finally moved to 148 Mercer Street and replaced by an 1896 building destined to become a Princeton landmark: Tudor Revival–style Lower Pyne.

Where Stockton Street branches off to the southwest from Nassau Street and Bayard Lane was once a parklike triangle with a beautiful line of venerable trees. Today the site holds the Princeton Borough Municipal Offices and the Princeton Battle Monument (under restoration as of 2006). But it is still a fine place for a leisurely weekend stroll, even if the passing automobiles have become more advanced and much more numerous.

Overlooking the little park and Stockton Street was the Princeton Inn, the town's finest late-19th-century hotel, shown here in 1896. In 1923, a new Princeton Inn was built on Alexander Street (now the Forbes undergraduate residential college of Princeton University). The old hotel became Miss Fine's School, an exclusive private secondary school for girls (also see page 50). It was torn down in 1965 to make way for today's Princeton Borough Hall.

Looking back eastwards from the previous locations, a row of houses can be seen that were also put to commercial uses. Surviving at the center, but without its old western addition, is 8 Stockton Street, today's Milholland and Olson Antiques and Interior Design Company.

The Corner Store (later the Farr Hardware Company) was a stalwart of trade to both borough dwellers and township farmers. The neighborhood near the intersection of Mercer Street (left) and Nassau Streets (right) had become more developed around 1834 when nearby Alexander Street was opened, encouraging more businesses on the western end of town. The store was torn down in September 1913, its bricks used to build a home for John S. Turney near Stony Brook. The semi-circular war memorial bench was dedicated in 1921 to the dead of World War I.

After the demise of the Corner Store, a vest pocket park was made possible by the relocation of the brick building that for years held Priest's Pharmacy (far right).

After World War I, a realignment of the head of Mercer Street and the creation of the French Market (where sales benefited French war relief) created today's layout.

The diagonal parking on Nassau Street lasted until after World War II. It was quite practical for its time, given the width of Princeton's main street and the relative narrowness of the era's motor vehicles.

The intersection of Nassau and Witherspoon Streets is the epicenter of Princeton. Here house movers are poised in 1901 to relocate the building on its west corner to a new location down Witherspoon Street. The five-story bank building that now stands on this spot was the first structure in town to have an elevator.

On the other corner of Nassau and Witherspoon Streets stands Lower Pyne, a jewel of Tudor Revival architecture. It was long a communications hub. It housed the Western Union telegraph office and was later a bus station. As seen here around 1920, it also once held the local post office. Trucks no longer pick up and deliver mail bags on its Witherspoon Street side. Today postal vehicles pass by and drive around the block to the local post office in Palmer Square or to the central office on Alexander Road.

The Central Hotel at 11 Witherspoon Street featured Franz Hill's Export Beer. Later acquired by the Dupraz family, it became the Dupraz Hotel and French restaurant, the forerunner of Lahiere's, Princeton's original fine dining destination.

A. Y. Stryker's steam, plumbing, and tinning business successfully served the town's demand for modern heating and home facilities. It moved from 12 John Street to this location at 30 Witherspoon Street around 1905–1908. The building, somewhat modified, is today the Alchemist and Barrister restaurant (so named because its founding partners were a pharmacist and an attorney).

Two trolley lines began carrying passengers and goods between the state capital of Trenton and Princeton around 1901. The fast line operated by the Trenton-Princeton Traction Company made the trip in about 35 minutes. It came up Witherspoon Street and first terminated on the site of today's Princeton Packet newspaper building. Later the line was extended to Spring Street (just beyond this intersection at Hulfish Street). It ceased operations in 1938, replaced by the cars, buses, and trucks that now roll on the streets.

Toto's Market at 74 Witherspoon Street, shown in April 1982, was for generations family-owned and customer-oriented, taking grocery orders and making three circuits of deliveries each day. The current occupant, the Witherspoon Bread Company, may not bring its delicious baked goods and coffees right to their customers front door, but it is no less a beloved, family-style shop.

In October 1913, three buildings were torn down to make way for the new Bickford Building at 116 Nassau Street (shown here in 1919). It opened on July 18, 1914. Among its tenants were a store of the Great Atlantic and Pacific Tea Company (later known as the A&P supermarket chain) and the Nassau Boot Shop. The structure was torn down in 1950 for a newer retail building, built with a Colonial Revival–style roof to hearken to Princeton's Colonial past. This was occupied for decades by a Woolworth's department store and, most recently, by children's and athletic clothing stores. As of 2006, an extensive academic and textbook store is planned for the building, continuing the site's history as a Nassau Street retail anchor.

The location of Margerum's Quarry on Ewing Street was the site of today's Quarry Park. Argillite, a slate-like stone from the Lockatong Formation underlying Princeton, was mined here. A similar operation closer to the center of town gave its name to Quarry Street.

Ed's Service Station at 249 Nassau Street, seen here in 1932, pumped three grades of Sinclair automotive gasoline. This charming stone building is gone, but the site still serves transportation as the home of Jay's Cycles.

The shops at 34–38 Alexander Street were part of a commercial sector serving a growing Princeton, among them a blacksmith's shop, carpenter, and meat market. The buildings were moved to make way for Payne Hall, an apartment building created in 1921 for missionaries on furlough as part of the Princeton Theological Seminary.

The Delaware and Raritan Canal, built in the 1830s and 1840s, was a commercial and transportation lifeline for New Jersey. Until it closed in 1932, it allowed direct navigation between the Delaware and Raritan Rivers, eliminating the long and hazardous voyage around Cape May. Ships such as the *Lottie B.* put into the Steamboat Hotel at Princeton Basin. Now a state park, the Delaware and Raritan Canal no longer supports vessels larger than canoes. The old hotel was torn down in July 1992 and was replaced by a private home.

Well into the 20th century, much land at the borough's edges was still agricultural. The Murphy place at today's 253 Witherspoon Street was being run by J. Golden Pierson as a dairy farm. In December 1918, prominent local businessman and developer Moses Taylor Pyne gave the five-acre property for the site of a new hospital. In 1952, during a hospital expansion, the old farmhouse was divided and moved to Arreton Road as two homes. As of 2006, there are plans to create a new facility for the still expanding medical center.

On a summer's day, the lake owned by the Princeton Ice Company gave little indication of the wintertime cutting and storing of ice blocks that preserved food in the days before widespread electric refrigeration. Today the site is the Mountain Lakes Preserve, a peaceful nature area in Princeton township.

Griggs Corner on Witherspoon Street was documented in 1983 by photographer and local historian Jeff Macechak. Long the site of the restaurant and home of Burnett Griggs. The Griggs Corner Amoco, one of the last gas stations in midtown, has given way to the Ichiban Japanese restaurant and UPS package shipping store.

Meanwhile behind the Griggs Corner Amoco was a park-and-shop lot. It has been converted to a sculpture and herb garden by the Mediterra Restaurant on nearby Hulfish Street.

As its girders rose on Harrison Street before its 1956 opening, the Princeton Shopping Center—the first of its kind in the region—was hailed as a dawning of postwar economic expansion. Anchored by a large Bamberger and Company department store, it had among its nearly 20 first tenants a bank, hardware store, two supermarkets, a laundromat, and a gas station. But some borough businessmen feared the center would drain customers from the downtown. In the 1970s, similar predictions were made about the Princeton Shopping Center's own future when the first major shopping malls were built along nearby Route 1. Today a reinvented shopping center still thrives and so does Princeton's downtown.

The aptly-named Route 1 stretches from Maine to Florida and, before the construction of Interstate 95, was the premiere driving route along the eastern United States. This section outside Princeton existed in the early 19th century. A major aspect of its widening and improvement in the 1930s was the installation of Jersey barriers to prevent head-on collisions. Today the Route 1 corridor and the office parks that have grown along it are synonymous with the Princeton area's leadership in business, research, and entrepreneurship.

HOMES HERE, GONE, OR JUST MOVED

RESIDENTIAL

Bainbridge House at 158 Nassau Street is a superb surviving mid-Georgian brick residence. Built about 1755–1760 by Job Stockton, it became closely associated with the Bainbridge family: Commodore William Bainbridge, commander of the frigate *Constitution* (nicknamed "Old Ironsides") in the War of 1812, was born here. It has been a physician's office, student boarding house, and public library. Since 1967, it has held the galleries and offices of the Historical Society of Princeton.

Morven on Stockton Street is perhaps Princeton's most historic house. The original structure was built in the 1750s by Richard Stockton (later a signer of the Declaration of Independence). It burned and was rebuilt about 1760. Stockton's poetess wife Annis Boudinot named it after a place in the lyrics of the mythical Scottish bard Ossian. In the latter 20th century, it was the official home of four New Jersey governors. After a recent loving restoration of its buildings and gardens, Morven looks much as it did in the 19th century, an embodiment of living Princeton history.

At the corner of Witherspoon and Wiggins Streets stood the home of the Wiggins family and the Old Parsonage. Their former occupants would scarcely recognize the location, now occupied by a power station and the Princeton Public Library.

Change with an abiding connection to history defines Princeton. Nowhere is this better shown than the intersection of Nassau and Harrison Streets, once the center of Queens Town, a settlement once separate from neighboring Prince Town. On the northwest corner, today's 342 Nassau Street is thought to have been built as early as 1730 by the Scott family. The wing on the right in the photograph taken around 1912 was moved to the building's west side when Harrison Street was widened in the late 1940s.

On the northeast corner of Nassau and Harrison Streets is 344 Nassau Street. Its left side also dates from the early 18th century. A full second story was added to it later. The larger main section, on the right, was built around 1824.

On the southeast corner, at 345 Nassau Street, underneath an early-20th-century stucco exterior, survives an 1830s-era building. For many years it was a Queens Town tavern. Around 1900, J. V. Fleming acquired this building for his grocery store. More recently, it has been occupied by realty firms.

Finally on the southwest corner at 341 Nassau Street, is Queen's Court, probably built in the late 18th century. John C. Shenck had a store and various other outbuildings here until 1836. At the time of the archival image, it was the Queenstown Girls Preparatory School. Its graduates studied across the street at Evelyn College for Women, which existed from 1888 to 1897.

In July 1906, during preparations for Princeton University's construction of Holder Hall, this 19th-century building was moved from its site next to the First Presbyterian Church to 12 Morven Place, where it stands today. The iron fence has a further Princeton University connection: it was made from the fencing that bordered the campus in front of Nassau Hall from 1838 to 1906.

A great period of Princeton University classroom and laboratory building along Washington Road in the late 1920s caused several homes to be razed or relocated.

The Olden-MacLaren House once stood at 38 Washington Street; it is now at 16 Boudinot Street.

A witness to ages of town history, this venerable residence once stood at 38 Stockton Street between Trinity Church and Thompson Hall. The core building may have been created in the 1830s by prominent Princeton carpenter, builder, and developer Charles Steadman, who was responsible for many homes in the neighborhood. It was an early home of Miss Fine's School and later served as a hospital during World War I and the flu pandemic of 1917. Now at 90 Westcott Road, it has been given a brick facade and its roofline has been much modified. Former New Jersey governor Richard Hughes lived here after his retirement.

The stately and spacious Andrew F. West house is shown around 1905 at its original location on Prospect Street at the corner of Washington Road. As private eating clubs organized by students grew and increased their social activities, many moved into new or existing houses on Prospect Street. West's home was acquired by the Campus Club.

In 1909, it was purchased by Moses Taylor Pyne and moved to its present location at 301 Nassau Street. The replacement Campus Club, shown in the modern image, was the work of prominent architect Raleigh C. Gildersleeve, designer of several notable town and campus structures.

Princeton University president James McCosh (1811–1894) retired to this beautiful house, seen around 1888 at its original Prospect Street location. In 1910, McCosh's house was acquired by the Quadrangle Club. In 1916, it was moved to 381 Nassau Street and in 1980, was converted into condominium units. Recently it has been lovingly renovated to again become a single private residence.

Vandeventer Street was named after the Dutch American family that operated a tree and plant nursery here. The neighborhood was developed in the late 1800s. These northward view shows that little has changed today, with the house built by John Topley around 1897 still at 32 Wiggins Street.

On the other side of town, Constitution Hill is thought to have been so named because the New Jersey state constitution was signed in this 18th-century farmhouse. The house was replaced in 1897 by the home of Junius Spencer Morgan, today part of the lovely Constitution Hill residential development.

HOMES HERE, GONE, OR JUST MOVED

Princeton University graduate and trustee Moses Taylor Pyne recognized that the school would need housing for its growing professorial ranks that was affordable but bespoke high social status. Around 1908, he constructed White City (so named because of its white, Tudor-style homes) just east of campus specifically for faculty and their families. At the corner of FitzRandolph Road and Western Way, the buildings have browned and the trees grown tall. But Pyne has given Princeton one of its most charming enclaves.

Meanwhile at the other end of the socioeconomic scale, John J. Golden saw a market for clean, simple housing for the workers in Nassau Street stores and warehouses. In 1909, he built Lincoln Court (known locally as Golden's Tenement) just off of Tulane Street. Except for the loss of its front porch, it looks the same today and is still valued by students and young workers for its relatively affordable apartments.

CHAPTER 3

BUILDING TOWARD THE ETERNAL
RELIGION

This Presbyterian chapel was built in 1880 by Rev. John Miller on the east side of Railroad Avenue (later University Place). It became a private home in 1901, its spire was removed and reinstalled on the Plainsboro Presbyterian Church. It was done away with during Princeton University dormitory building in 1914.

The Princeton meetinghouse of the Society of Friends (Quaker) has changed little since it was built in 1759 to replace a 1724 building badly damaged by fire. The present structure may be nearly identical to the original, but the surrounding countryside has changed greatly, having gone from open farmland back to woodland. A successful Quaker grade school now also operates on the property and is attended by youngsters of many religious backgrounds, continuing the Society of Friends' tradition of community improvement through education.

Like the estate of Morven (page 42), the Nassau Presbyterian Church at 61 Nassau Street is a seemingly timeless Princeton building. A church first opened on this site in 1766. The congregation rebuilt after two fires. The current structure (seen in this archival photograph from sometime before 1876) today looks, from this angle, much as it did when it was erected in 1836.

The Princeton United Methodist Church was built in 1849 on Nassau Street and stood with its parsonage next door on the corner of Vandeventer Street. They were replaced in 1909 by today's larger, classically-styled church, with the parsonage moved to 25 Vandeventer Street.

BUILDING TOWARDS THE ETERNAL

The Episcopal church was slow to become established in Princeton, in part because many of its Anglican adherents had been loyalists during the American Revolution. But an Episcopal parish was formed in 1827, and work on its first building started five years later. The Trinity Parish School was built in 1849. Both white apprentices and black children were educated here. Originally a freestanding building, it survives as a wing of the Trinity Church complex.

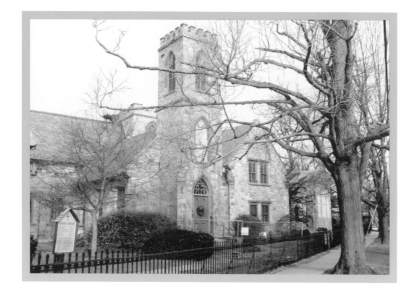

Mass was celebrated in Princeton as early as 1795. The first Catholic church was built at 182 Nassau Street in 1850. The Church of St. Paul, seen here in the archival photograph, dates from 1869 with a new facade added in 1912. The church and its rectory were later used to create houses on nearby Charlton Street. The present Church of St. Paul, located at 214 Nassau Street, was dedicated in 1957.

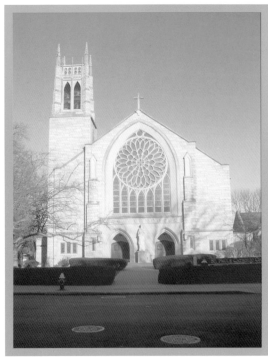

The Princeton Theological Seminary was founded in 1811. Its chapel was built in 1833 and originally faced north toward Mercer Street. In 1934, it was moved back and rotated to the west. Today the chapel and later neighboring buildings help define a lovely interior campus for the seminary.

The Bright Hope Baptist Church was organized in 1885. Its predominately African American congregation built the church (shown in a 1950s archival photograph) on a plot of land it had purchased on John Street at the corner of Green Street. John Street no longer runs past its entrance, having been rerouted with the opening of the thoroughfare that is today known as Paul Robeson Place. In the 1930s, the church was renovated and renamed the First Baptist Church. Its strong and striking facade came with an expansion and further renovation in 1968. (Vintage image courtesy of Shirley Satterfield.)

There have been several chapels in Princeton University history. A small prayer hall was included in Nassau Hall when it opened in 1756. A separate chapel was built in 1847. That was superseded in 1882 by the glorious Marquand Chapel (seen here, with Murray-Dodge Hall on the right). When nearby Dickinson Hall caught fire in 1920, sparks ignited the roof timbers of Marquand Chapel, causing its loss as well. Today its site is an open space between Murray-Dodge and the current university chapel (at left, dedicated in 1928).

In 1926, a humble upstairs room in the Branch Building on Witherspoon Street became the meeting place for Congregation B'nai Zion. The congregation later moved around the corner to a storefront (shown here) at 9 Spring Street. The meeting rooms of the Jewish Center of Princeton were begun at 457 Nassau Street in 1956. The center has been expanded over the years to become today's spacious and inspiring site for religious, educational, and social activities.

CHAPTER 4

A TIMELESS AND CHANGING CAMPUS

PRINCETON UNIVERSITY

Prospect Street is framed by the arch of 1879 Hall, given in 1904 by the famed undergraduate class whose members included Woodrow Wilson. Outside on the right reclines one of a pair of lions that the class of 1879 originally gave for Nassau Hall (these were replaced by tiger statues; the lions now guard Wilcox Hall).

When it opened in November 1756, Nassau Hall reputedly was the largest stone building in North America. It was 177 feet long and about 54 feet wide, with three stories and a basement. It contained the entire College of New Jersey: its "recitation rooms" (classrooms), library, prayer hall, kitchen, and dining facilities, plus lodgings for some 150 students and instructors. Its walls, built of local sandstone, survived two devastating fires (the second in 1855 leading to the most significant modifications in its architecture). It has undergone a number of repairs and modifications and today houses the school's top administrators. Its nickname "Old Nassau" is synonymous with Princeton University itself. (Engraving reproduced by permission of the Princeton University Library.)

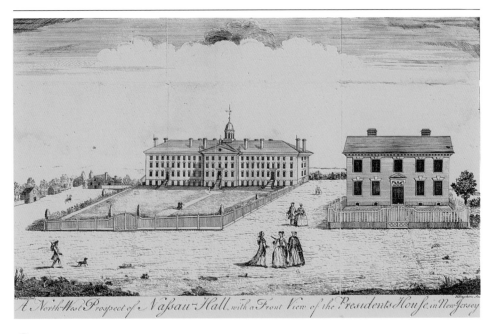

A North-West Prospect of Nassau-Hall, with a Front View of the Presidents House, in New-Jersey

A fire swept Nassau Hall in 1802, leaving only its thick walls standing. It was rebuilt by renowned architect Benjamin Henry Latrobe, later to do significant work on the United States Capitol Building. At that time, Latrobe also designed Stanhope Hall and its twin, Philosophical Hall. The latter, shown in the archival image, was razed in 1873 to make room for the Chancellor Green Library, partly seen in the modern view. The Henry House (modern view, left) was built by scientist-professor Joseph Henry in 1837. It has been moved around campus three times, coming to rest here in 1947 to make room for nearby Firestone Library.

Another terrible fire burned Nassau Hall in 1855. This rear view was taken after John Notman restored it, adding end stairwell towers, a larger bell cupola and an elongated south wing. The original chapel (on the right of the archival photograph) was taken down in 1897 to make way for East Pyne Hall (erected on the site where the photographer had stood). The ornate belvederes of Nassau Hall's stair towers were removed in 1905. The tree in the center, now long gone, was nicknamed the "Bulletin Elm," used for posting announcements.

The Osborn Field House was named after prominent Princeton University trustee and benefactor Henry Fairfield Osborn, class of 1877. It was built in the late 19th century in the southwest corner of the athletic fields at the intersection of Olden and Prospect Streets. The sports competitions moved elsewhere in the early 20th century, and on the old fields now stand the Engineering Quadrangle and a parking garage. But the field house has a new life as the Carl A. Fields Center for Equality and Cultural Understanding.

As its name suggests, the Observatory of Instruction was a teaching, not research, facility. The associated house was the residence of the head of the astronomy department. It was torn down in 1963, giving way to the new universe of Robertson Hall at the Woodrow Wilson School of Public and International Affairs (above in the modern view, dedicated in 1966) and, eventually, Bendheim Hall (1991).

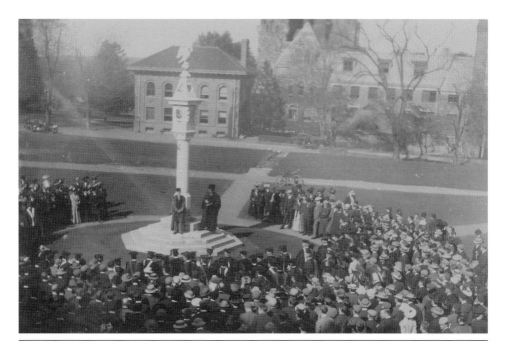

An admirer of British universities while president of Princeton, Woodrow Wilson welcomed the 1907 donation by Sir William Mather of a replica of the famed 1551 sundial of Corpus Christi College, Oxford. Behind it stands the 1877 Biology Laboratory (left, torn down in 1946 to make room for Firestone Library) and the John C. Green School of Science building (right, burned down 1928). Today the stalwart yet soaring Princeton University Chapel defines the northern edge of the Mather Sundial courtyard.

Blair Hall, with its distinctive archway, was built in 1897 to present an impressive castlelike greeting to visitors arriving by train. Today looking back out through the arch, the train station is gone, replaced by dormitories and the Princeton University Store.

University Place was once known as Railroad Avenue due to the branch line that carried freight and passengers to the town and campus. This particular train was a special one, used by Princeton University trustee Moses Taylor Pyne and his business associates to commute north to Manhattan. In 1918, the track's terminus was moved about a quarter mile south and a smaller depot built there.

The moving of the station was part of an overall plan to erect new dormitories and other buildings along University Place. The homes in the archival photograph were moved or razed at about that time.

The second building from the left in the modern view, a former private dormitory, is now home to the *Daily Princetonian*, the campus newspaper.

A TIMELESS AND CHANGING CAMPUS

Before the building of Palmer Stadium in 1914, these lower campus fields saw many exciting football matchups. They were also a parade ground during World War I training. Here in 1923 was opened Baker Rink, America's first collegiate indoor rink, named after legendary Princeton University hockey player Hobey Baker, class of 1917. Behind it rises the impressive Whitman residential college, a major Collegiate Gothic structure scheduled for opening in the fall of 2007.

When the Princeton University Gymnasium was constructed in 1903, it was the largest such facility in America. It was the center of Princeton University's varsity athletics until its destruction by a fire in 1944. Dillon Gymnasium, completed in 1947, was purposely designed to hearken to its predecessor. Seen in the left background of the archival image is the Brokaw Memorial Building, which contained an indoor swimming pool. As Dillon Gymnasium was being built with a major new pool, the old Brokaw Memorial Building was torn down.

CHAPTER

5

PRINCETON'S
VILLAGE GREEN

THE DEVELOPMENT
OF PALMER SQUARE

If not the crossroads of Princeton, Palmer Square became its crosswalk. On a sunny spring day in the early 1960s, a sign pointed the way to destinations while shirt-sleeved citizens strolled Nassau Street. Tudor Revival–style Upper Pyne Hall still lent its Elizabethan elegance but would be torn down in the summer of 1963 for a bank and office building.

In 1925, businessman-developer and Princeton graduate Edger Palmer began buying up buildings on this section of Nassau Street with plans to create a commercial and apartment district surrounding a square. The gap between the buildings is the southern end of John Street.

No project changed the face of the town as did Palmer Square. The Great Depression delayed the first stage of the work until 1936 (with completion in 1941), but the project also significantly helped Princeton with new jobs and commerce.

The original Nassau Inn was perhaps the most historic of the buildings razed to open Nassau Street for the square. Defenders of the project insisted that the structure was seriously dilapidated and little remained of the original 18th-century inn that stood on the site. Its famous sign was rescued and now proudly advertises the modern Nassau Inn outside its eastern lobby entrance.

Upper Pyne and Lower Pyne buildings were designed by Raleigh G. Gildersleeve. They were named after Moses Taylor Pyne, who constructed Tudor Revival buildings in town to compliment the campus's Collegiate Gothic structures. They held street level businesses and upper floor student rooms. Upper Pyne, shown here, opened in December 1896. The small archway on the left was the entrance to Baker Alley, all gone now.

These contrasting views of the north side of Nassau Street taken from the university campus—one taken in 1897, one contemporary—show what a dramatic effect the Palmer Square project had on the townscape of Princeton.

PALMER SQUARE OFFICE BUILDING,
PRINCETON, N.J.
CHARLES K. AGLE, ARCHITECT,
WM. L. CROW CONSTRUCTION CO.
VIEW LOOKING-NE
NO. 1 DATE 7-9-63

A diagonal view of the southeast corner of the Palmer Square complex was taken in July 1963 just before the demolition of Upper Pyne to make way for the bank, office, and retail buildings that stand there today. The newspaper kiosk was added in the 1980s.

A remarkable series of photographs taken in the late 1920s has documented the neighborhood replaced by Palmer Square. Here Baker Alley is seen looking north from Nassau Street. Today the street is Palmer Square East and spanned by a walkway connecting wings of the Nassau Inn.

PRINCETON'S VILLAGE GREEN

This is Baker Alley looking south to Nassau Street from Hulfish Street. Several homes on the right were moved to Birch Avenue. Families affected by the project in this predominately African American neighborhood relocated to new dwellings.

John Street, originally called Johns Alley, is believed to have been named after resident John Scudder. It is shown in the photographs looking north from Nassau Street. The Princeton newspaper distribution service is on the right. Today this section of John Street is used only as an alleyway behind Palmer Square West.

Further north down John Street was found the old Princeton Rug Washing and Carpet Cleaning Works. Today's shops along Palmer Square West are attractive but probably could never be as colorfully expansive as this vanished business.

Looking back south on John Street old residences are seen at the intersection of Hulfish Street, but today on the right is a parking garage. However, John Street continues several blocks away in the north part of town as part of a still-vital residential neighborhood.

Hulfish Street runs between John and Witherspoon Streets, with these views, taken eastward to Witherspoon Street. The front porch of Mame Keys (left) was renowned for its lush covering of vines. Hulfish Street now defines Palmer Square North.

Jackson Street also ran between John and Witherspoon Streets. The archival view, looking eastward, reveals a charming neighborhood with homes unlike the dilapidated dwellings replaced by Palmer Square. The first house on the left belonged to George Macon, a successful taxi service owner. The site was once occupied by the Princeton Playhouse (see page 94) and today by the shops and parking garage of Palmer Square North.

Given Princeton's history as a stagecoach town, it is not surprising that behind the original Nassau Inn was a complex of stables (including Bergen's Stables, left) and later, garages (such as the Princeton Garage, right, run for many years by Jack Mooney). Today this approximate area contains the reinvented Nassau Inn (left) and the Princeton post office (right).

The Princeton Playhouse was a true entertainment destination. Even Albert Einstein enjoyed Saturday matinees there. In 1942, when it was only four years old, its marquee advertised a movie mystery. But it is no mystery why in 1981 the Princeton Playhouse was torn down and its parking lot torn up for new offices, shops, and restaurants along Hulfish Street. Large single-screen movie houses were no longer economically viable in the era of television and home videos.

Critics of the 1963 construction of 1 Palmer Square maintained that its contemporary architecture subverted the square's original 18th- and 19th-century-revival concept (shown in this architect's drawing, around 1938). Its aesthetics are still debated, but thanks to recent renovations Palmer Square continues as a solid commercial success, bolstering the downtown business district and helping assure many "nows" in Princeton's future.

Across America, People are Discovering Something Wonderful. *Their Heritage.*

Arcadia Publishing is the leading local history publisher in the United States. With more than 3,000 titles in print and hundreds of new titles released every year, Arcadia has extensive specialized experience chronicling the history of communities and celebrating America's hidden stories, bringing to life the people, places, and events from the past. To discover the history of other communities across the nation, please visit:

www.arcadiapublishing.com

Customized search tools allow you to find regional history books about the town where you grew up, the cities where your friends and family live, the town where your parents met, or even that retirement spot you've been dreaming about.